HOW RENEWABLE ENERGY WORKS

Geoff Barker

W

FRANKLIN WATTS
LONDON • SYDNEY

First published in 2015 by Franklin Watts
338 Euston Road
London NW1 3BH

Franklin Watts Australia
Level 17/207 Kent Street
Sydney, NSW 2000

Produced by Calcium

A CIP catalogue record for this book is available from
the British Library.

ISBN 978 1 4451 3903 6

Dewey classification: 333.7'94

Printed in China

Franklin Watts is a division of Hachette Children's Books, an Hachette UK company
www.hachette.co.uk

Acknowledgements:
The publisher would like to thank the following for permission to reproduce photographs:
Cover: Shutterstock: Esbobeldijk fg, WDG Photo bg. Inside: Pelamiswave.com: 1, 19;
Shutterstock: Bahri Altay 15, Constantine Androsoff 16, Bikeworldtravel 7, Jack Cronkhite
29, Iain Frazer 9, Jason and Bonnie Grower 26, Jimmi 13, Zoran Karapancev 27, Denis
Kichatof 20, Kletr 5, Kzenon 12, Majeczka 6, Maximillion69 11, Meanmachine77 17, Bas
Meelker 24, N.Minton 21, Beneda Miroslav 18, Nostal6iec 22, Num Skyman 4, Pics-xl 14,
Daniel Prudek 2, 23, Moreno Soppelsa 25, Silver Tiger 8, Vaclav Volrab 28.

Every attempt has been made to clear copyright. Should there be any inadvertent
omission please apply to the publisher for rectification.

Contents

Rethinking energy 4

Renewable energy 6

Power from the sun 8

Solar cells 10

Solar developments 12

Wind power 14

Moving water 16

Tides and waves 18

Heat from the Earth 20

Biomass 22

Biogas 24

Fuel cells 26

What next? 28

Glossary 30

For more information 31

Index 32

Rethinking energy

What do you know about energy? You need energy to run, throw a ball and swim. Energy is also what makes plants grow, and what powers our cars, computers and factories.

What are our energy sources?

We get our own energy from the food we eat. Light and heat energy is available directly from the sun. We can also get energy to power machines and to make electricity from fossil fuels such as oil, coal and natural gas. These types of energy are called non-renewable energy resources, because they are finite. This means that they will run out.

We build offshore oil rigs to get oil from under the oceans. Oil is a non-renewable energy resource.

Nuclear power stations harness the energy from nuclear reactions. When two nuclear particles collide it creates a reaction that gives off energy.

ECO FACT

Running out

Many people are worried about what is going to happen when oil, coal and gas supplies run out. At the moment we rely on them, but we need to rethink where we get energy from and how we use it. This book is about energy sources that will never run out – renewable energy.

What about nuclear energy?

Nuclear power stations were once seen by many as the answer to our energy problems. However, there are risks involved in creating nuclear power. For example, the waste products are harmful to humans and the environment. Today, many people think that nuclear energy raises too many problems to be a practical, long-term energy source.

Renewable energy

Large wind turbines are built to exploit the naturally occurring, renewable resource of wind.

We can get renewable energy from all sorts of places, such as the sun, the wind and moving water. We can even get energy from animal manure. These energy sources will always be available to us. The energy of the future is likely to come from a mixture of many types of renewable energy resources.

Stop global warming

Fossil fuels are energy sources that will eventually run out, but they also have another big drawback. Fossil fuels are harmful to the environment. They are causing global warming and changing our climate. Renewable energy resources either emit no greenhouse gases (GHGs) or they are emissions-neutral over their lifetime. Emissions-neutral means that the harm something does is balanced out by its positive impact.

Pedal power is a great way to travel and does not harm the environment.

Converting renewable energy

Renewable energy resources need to be converted, or changed, before we can use them. Most of the energy we use to power our machines and buildings is electricity. Different renewable energy resources can be converted to generate, or make, electricity. Some forms of renewable energy are more efficient than others. This means that there is very little waste.

What is global warming?

When fossil fuels are burnt, they release harmful gases, including sulphur dioxide (which creates acid rain) and carbon dioxide, which is a GHG.

- Like glass in a greenhouse for plants, GHGs keep the Earth warm.
- Burning fossil fuels increases the amount of GHGs.
- GHGs are causing world temperatures to rise.
- The rise in world temperatures is known as global warming and it is causing climate change.

Power from the sun

The sun is a natural source of light and heat energy, known as solar energy. It keeps our planet warm enough for life to exist. We can use its heat energy to heat air and water. Light energy can also generate electricity.

Passive solar design

Through improved design, we can make greater use of the sun's heat. Solar energy can warm a building if the sun shines through large south-facing windows. Walls painted black trap heat well, as dark surfaces absorb heat energy much better than light surfaces. This is passive solar design.

All living things on the planet – animals, plants and you – depend on the sun's energy to stay alive.

ECO FACT

Great ball of energy

The sun is a giant ball of hot gases with a surface temperature of up to 5,500 °C. Although only a small fraction of the sun's energy reaches Earth, this is still enough to supply the whole world's energy needs – if we could capture it and use it efficiently.

Heating water

You can also use solar energy to heat water. Solar panels can be fitted to the roof of a house. They have a flat, clear glass top, then a dark metal plate underneath that absorbs the heat from the sun. Water flows through the panels, where it is warmed up by the sun's heat energy.

Making electricity

At solar power stations, the sun's light energy is used to generate electricity. Reflectors are used to direct sunlight onto water. The energy boils the water, making steam that then runs turbines, which generate electricity.

A giant reflector dish at a solar power station in France collects the sun's powerful rays.

Solar cells

You may not know this, but you have probably used a solar cell before. Most pocket calculators are powered by energy from small solar cells. These cells use technology called photovoltaics (PV) to convert light energy into electrical energy. They are a 'green' (environmentally friendly) energy source.

PV cells in solar panels convert the energy of the sun into electricity.

Photovoltaic technology

PV cells were invented in the 1960s in the United States and used by engineers to provide power for satellites in space. These cells are much larger than the ones used to power calculators! PV cells are now being used for a variety of purposes. Photovoltaics can be a very efficient way of providing electricity to remote, sunny locations that are not connected to an electricity grid. PV cells also work well in cloudy regions, such as northern Europe and parts of North America.

PV solar panels

Most of the PV solar panels in use today can convert only around 10 per cent of the sun's light energy that reaches them into electricity. They are also costly because they are made of silicon cells, which are expensive. A new type of cell, called a thin-film solar cell, is also now available. This uses copper, indium, gallium and selenide (or CIGS for short) instead of silicon. It is cheaper to produce than a silicon cell.

Even the best solar panels are only approximately 20 per cent efficient.

PV cells up close

PV cells generate electricity directly from sunlight. Cells use layers of silicon as a semi-conductor. Sunlight strikes the PV cell and electrical charges pass between the layers to produce an electric current. PV cells have no moving parts, so they are silent and they need little maintenance.

11

Solar developments

Will a car or a plane ever run on sunlight? You might be surprised to discover that both have happened already. Scientists are researching all sorts of exciting developments using solar energy.

Solar transport

A car of the future could be powered by solar cells on its surface, instead of petrol or diesel. There are experimental solar-powered cars already, but they are not yet as practical or affordable as regular cars. Car manufacturers will make 'green' cars only if enough people want to buy them. NASA (National Aeronautics and Space Administration) is researching alternative options for powering planes. NASA has tested Helios, an unmanned 'flying wing', in 2001 – it was powered by solar energy.

Will filling up a car at a petrol station be such a common sight in the future?

ECO FACT

Solar paint

Researchers are looking into the possibility of using solar paint on the surfaces of buildings. The paint contains special semi-conductive particles that work in a similar way to PV cell panels. The particles could capture sunlight, which could then be turned into electricity. The technology requires less space than solar panels, and is very cheap and simple. However, solar paint needs to be more efficient to be a practical option.

Solar power stations in space

Teams of aerospace engineers in Japan, the United States and Europe are currently working on plans to launch a solar power station into space. In space, the solar power station would not be affected by clouds and it would be much closer to the sun. The satellite would be covered with solar panels. Electricity could be transmitted to Earth in the form of microwaves or lasers, then passed along cables to its destination.

Solar panels on a satellite in space convert the sun's energy into electricity.

13

Wind power

When the sun heats up the land, the air above rises and cool air comes to take its place. This movement is what we know as 'wind'. Wind energy can be used to drive different types of machines, or it can be turned into electricity. Wind is a clean energy, which means it does not give off pollution. It is also renewable.

Wind turbines

Most wind turbines have two or three thin blades, like aeroplane propellers, mounted at the top of a tall tower about 60 metres high. When the blades spin, they turn the generator, which makes electricity.

The wind is stronger higher above the ground, so wind turbines are getting taller and taller. So far the tallest turbine tower built is around 160 metres above the ground, and the blade tips reach up to a height of 205 metres!

Wind turbines built by the coast make the most of typical windy conditions.

14

Wind turbines up close

There are two main designs of wind turbine: horizontal axis or vertical axis turbines. The horizontal axis turbines are a tall vertical tower with a drive shaft set behind rotating blades. The drive shaft connects to the generator at the top of the tower. Vertical axis turbines have very long, curved blades that reach from the top of the turbine tower to the bottom, bowing out in the middle. They work when the wind is blowing in any direction.

A horizontal axis turbine is set at the very top of a tall tower – behind the large blades.

Are there any drawbacks?

Wind turbines are currently quite expensive to build, although once the turbines have been built, running costs are low. Wind turbines also cannot work if the wind is too strong.

Many people argue that wind farms spoil views of the countryside. They can also be surprisingly noisy, so wind turbines are often placed in remote areas. Some wind farms have even been built out at sea. These are known as offshore wind farms. However, they are a lot more expensive to build.

Moving water

Humans have used water power for thousands of years. As far back as 3,000 years ago, people used water wheels on rivers. They used the energy of the water to grind corn and create irrigation systems to water crops.

Hydroelectric power

Today, we use the energy in moving water to drive electricity generators. This is called hydroelectric power (HEP), which is based on the simple idea that water flows from high to low places. Falling water releases energy that can then be captured and used to generate electricity. The water is contained in a large lake, or reservoir, held back by a huge barrier, called a dam. The technology of HEP is clean and it is a renewable type of energy. The first hydroelectric dam appeared towards the end of the nineteenth century, and today HEP is used all over the world.

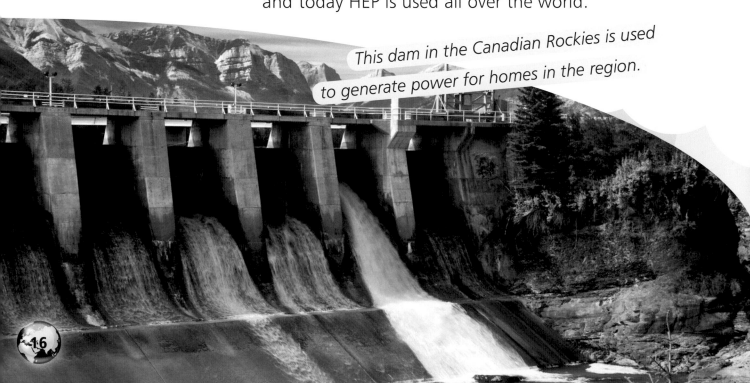

This dam in the Canadian Rockies is used to generate power for homes in the region.

For and against

Hydroelectric dams and power stations cost a lot to build, but HEP is very efficient. It converts around 90 per cent of the water's energy directly into electricity. However, there are several drawbacks to HEP. Often vast areas of land need to be flooded to create the reservoir, sometimes forcing large numbers of people to move from their homes. In China, more than 1.2 million people were forced to move to make way for the building of the massive Three Gorges Dam. Reservoirs and dams also alter the natural flow of rivers, and the whole ecological system of a region can be badly affected.

China's Three Gorges Dam is the biggest ever hydroelectric dam.

ECO FACT

How hydroelectric dams work

Dams are built to create reservoirs, or large lakes, of water. The dams hold back the water, then release it into pipes with turbines inside. The turbines often look like ships' propellers and they spin around due to the force of the water passing through them. The turbines are connected to a power station containing electricity generators.

Tides and waves

When waves crash into rocks they show just how powerful they are.

We can capture energy from all sorts of moving water – including tides and waves. The movement of the water can be converted into energy. This is a clean and renewable source of energy, because tides and waves are the natural behaviour of our oceans.

Tidal barrages

On the part of Earth closest to the moon, there is a high tide. Elsewhere on Earth, the sea level goes down and the tide is low. The energy from these changes in sea level can be captured and used to generate electricity. This is done by building long tidal barriers, called barrages. Sea water is let in and out through pipes in the tidal barrage. The water turns turbines inside the pipes, which turn generators to create electricity. Only certain places are suitable for building tidal barrages, such as La Rance, in France.

Wave energy

Surfers know all about the energy of waves. No waves, no surfing! Waves are produced by the action of the wind blowing across the oceans. Although there is a vast amount of energy in waves, it is quite difficult to harness. Two types of wave machine have been developed to do this job – floating and fixed.

The Pelamis wave machine is a floating device that captures energy from waves off the coast of Orkney, Scotland.

Wave energy up close

Floating wave machines are positioned on the surface of the sea, and bob up and down like buoys. This wave energy turns a generator that converts it into electricity. One example is known as Salter's Duck – British designer Stephen Salter designed his 'duck' to nod up and down as waves pass.

Fixed wave machines are located on the coast or anchored to the seabed. The wave power is used to compress air, which drives a turbine to generate electricity. Fixed devices are used in countries with rough seas such as Britain and Portugal.

Heat from the Earth

Far, far below us in the centre of the Earth is a fireball with temperatures of up to 7,000 °C. The natural heat from the hot water and rock found beneath the Earth's surface is called geothermal energy, meaning 'heat energy from the Earth'.

Iceland's impressive geysers demonstrate geothermal energy.

Hot water

Certain volcanic areas, such as Iceland, New Zealand and parts of North America, have hot rocks lying close to the surface of the Earth. The warmth from these rocks heats up surface waters to create hot springs. The heated water can be pumped out and used directly to provide heat to nearby buildings.

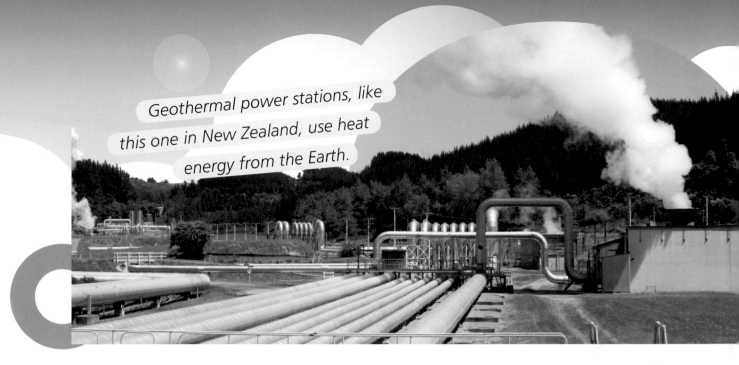

Geothermal power stations, like this one in New Zealand, use heat energy from the Earth.

Green Iceland

In Iceland, about 85 per cent of the population uses geothermal heat in this way. Geothermal power stations are also built close to the hot water springs, using the naturally occurring steam to spin turbines for electricity. In many geothermal power stations, once the heat is used, the cooled water is recycled.

Hot rocks

Another way of using geothermal heat is to pump cold water at pressure through cracks in hot, dry rocks. The water heats up and is pumped back to the surface.

Heat pumps up close

Just under the surface of the Earth, the temperature stays fairly constant throughout the year. A geothermal heat pump system exploits the difference between the air and the ground.

- During the winter, heat pumps remove heat from the ground and transfer it to buildings.
- During the summer, heat is taken out of buildings and pumped into the ground to cool the buildings.
- In summer or winter, heated water in the system can also be used.

Biomass

Photosynthesis is the process by which plants make food using light energy from the sun. When we burn plants, they release stored chemical energy. This energy can be used to make heat and electricity. This is biomass energy.

Biomass fuel

The most widespread biomass fuel is wood. People have been burning wood and dried vegetation for hundreds of thousands of years. Biomass energy is still the main source of energy for millions of people, particularly in poorer countries. Burning wood is more difficult than burning fossil fuels but it is not as harmful to the environment. As trees grow, they add oxygen and take carbon dioxide out of the atmosphere. When trees are burnt, they put back the same amount of carbon dioxide, so overall there is no change in the balance of the gas in the atmosphere.

A biomass power plant uses wood chips as its source of fuel.

Crops of bright-yellow oilseed rape can be used to replace diesel to fuel cars.

Raw materials

Fast-growing trees, such as willows and poplars, are often grown for biomass fuel. They can be harvested and burnt in a furnace about four years after planting. Small pieces of wood burn much better than big logs, so power stations often use wood chips as the most efficient form of biomass fuel.

Ethanol and biodiesel

Plants such as oilseed rape are very rich in oil. They can be turned into a liquid fuel called biodiesel. Sugar cane can be fermented to produce a colourless liquid called ethanol, a type of alcohol. These fuels can be used as a substitute for diesel and petrol in vehicles.

ECO FACT

Converting the power of the sun

Ultimately, the sun is responsible for all sorts of energy, including biomass. Green plants need sunlight to grow. In photosynthesis, plants take in the raw materials of water and carbon dioxide. They then use the energy in the sun's rays to turn the materials into sugars, to help the plants to grow. We eat the plants for energy, or burn them for biomass energy.

Biogas

You may ask, what is animal manure good for? Quite a lot, actually! As it begins to rot, manure gives off a gas called methane. This is biogas and it is a very useful source of energy.

Rotting biomass

As animal and plant waste (or biomass) rots, methane is generated. This biogas is a useful fuel substitute for natural gas. A way to capture the gas emitted from rotting waste has been developed. It is called a digester. Capturing methane in this way is useful and beneficial, as methane is one of the harmful GHGs responsible for global warming.

The average dairy cow produces more than 40 kilograms of manure every day, as well as plenty of methane.

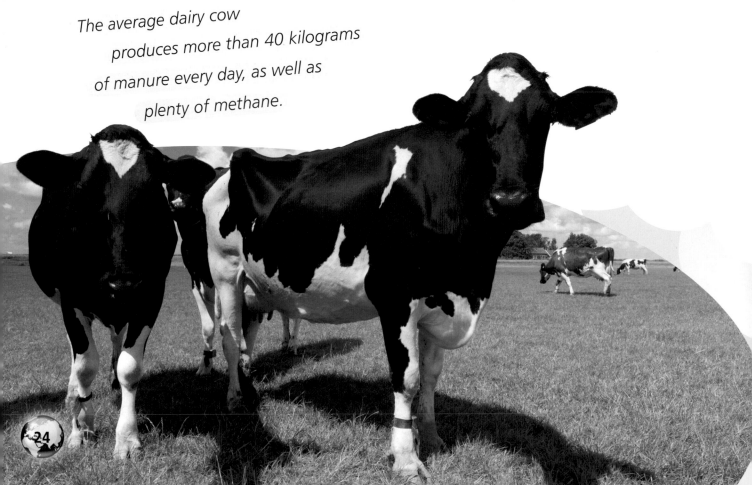

Help on the farm

The use of digesters is particularly suitable in countries and regions where intensive farming is common, and large quantities of waste are produced. If the manure is put into digesters, the biogas produced can then be used for fuel, for example to power a generator for electricity. Once the biogas has been extracted, the remaining solids can then be used as a natural fertiliser.

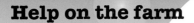

Making use of rotting biomass, the commercial production of biogas continues to grow.

Digesters up close

All sorts of human and animal waste, including manure, can be put into a special tank called a digester, which captures the methane gas, so it can be used.

- Waste matter is starved of oxygen.
- Naturally occurring bacteria ferment the waste.
- As the matter rots, it releases gases, including methane.
- Methane is piped away, for use as a fuel in heating and cooking.

Fuel cells

A fuel cell is very similar to a large battery, converting chemical energy into electrical energy. Fuel cells combine hydrogen and oxygen to generate electricity and heat. Water is then produced as a harmless by-product.

Starting with hydrogen

Hydrogen is the most abundant element in the universe. It has great potential as a future energy source. Hydrogen has already been used as a fuel to launch rockets and space shuttles. Although hydrogen is present in our atmosphere, it needs extracting before we can use it. Most of the hydrogen we use is produced by extracting it from fossil fuels, such as natural gas (made up of hydrogen and carbon). This uses up great quantities of energy, so it is not sustainable.

Shuttles used hydrogen as a fuel to power them into space.

Applications of fuel cells

Fuel cells are able to convert energy into electricity more efficiently than other power sources. Fuel cells are currently being developed to work with an electric motor in a vehicle. A fuel cell for a car is twice as efficient as a petrol engine, with the added advantage that there is practically no pollution! One of the major drawbacks is that fuel cells are expensive to produce.

The way forward?

Water is made up of oxygen and hydrogen. By using a process called electrolysis, it can be split into hydrogen and oxygen. However, a large amount of electricity is needed to carry out electrolysis. If this electricity came from a renewable source, such as wind or solar, fuel cells would become a truly sustainable energy form.

The recent Mazda RX-8 Hydrogen RE car runs on hydrogen.

ECO FACT

How fuel cells work

A fuel cell is a box that converts energy. Hydrogen, the fuel, enters at one electrode, with oxygen entering at the other. The two elements react, producing an electric current. The waste product is water.

What next?

We know that fossil fuels will not last forever, but the world's demands for energy are constantly increasing as our planet's population grows. Renewable energy sources, including biomass, solar, wind and water energy, must all play a part in meeting our huge energy needs in the future.

Still relying on oil?

It makes sense for us to use alternative energy sources, but we shall also continue to rely on non-renewable fossil fuels for as long as possible. The oil industry, for example, is developing new methods to extract oil that is difficult to reach, such as oil found deep beneath the seabed or beneath very thick ice.

Solar energy panels can efficiently provide electricity to more remote locations.

ECO FACT

Energy efficiency

Today, most renewable energy comes from burning biomass, but the future will see rises in the use of other sources, including solar power and geothermal energy. Important savings of energy can also lie in energy efficiency. At home, we can replace traditional light bulbs with energy-efficient lights. We can also buy energy-efficient electrical appliances. New building standards could also enforce the heating efficiency of homes and businesses. We are now looking towards a future of using less and conserving more.

Car designers continue to research alternative forms of energy – including solar-powered cars.

Alternative energy grows

We know that renewable energy sources will always be around for as long as the sun's rays reach our planet. By 2040, about 15 per cent of the world's energy will come from renewable sources. It is necessary to move away from our dependence on fossil fuels and make the most of renewable energy resources.

Glossary

acid rain acidic rainfall that can damage living things and even buildings

alternative energy types of renewable energy

biogas a gas, such as methane, that is produced when living things rot

biomass fuel matter from living things used as fuel

by-product something extra that is produced

chemical energy the stored energy in chemicals

dam a barrier built across a river or lake to hold back water

digester a device used to collect methane from rotting animal waste

ecological to do with the relationship between organisms and their environment

efficiency functioning well with very little waste

electric current the movement or flow of electrical charge

electrode a wire or rod conductor through which electric current enters or leaves during the process of electrolysis

electrolysis a process in which an electric current passes through a liquid

emissions-neutral when harmful emissions are balanced out by positive emissions

extracted removed

ferment to cause a chemical reaction (called fermentation)

finite limited

fossil fuels fuels such as oil made from the remains of dead organisms

generator a machine used to produce electricity

harness to gain control of

intensive farming producing large amounts of crops

irrigation a method of supplying an area with water

natural gas a gas that is found on Earth and that is not man-made

non-renewable will run out

photosynthesis a process in which plants make food using light energy from the sun

photovoltaics (PV) a technology converting the sun's light energy into electrical energy

react to have a reaction, or response, to something

renewable will not run out and can be replaced

reservoir a large lake behind a dam

satellites spacecraft that orbit Earth

semi-conductor a substance, such as silicon, which can conduct electricity under some conditions (but is not a true conductor like copper)

silicon a chemical element (found in sand) that is a semi-conductor

solar to do with the sun

solar panel a panel that absorbs and uses the sun's heat energy

sustainable able to keep going

tidal barrages barriers across an expanse of water where tides flow

turbines machines that turn by water, steam or air

30

For more information

Books

A Refreshing Look at Renewable Energy With Max Axiom, Super Scientist, Katherine Krohn, Capstone

Energy (Eyewitness), Jack Challoner, DK Publishing

Power for the Planet (Our Green Earth), Anne Flounders, Red Chair Press

Water Power (Looking at Energy), Polly Goodman, Wayland

Websites

Try out the games and activities on the 'Energy Kids' website at:
www.eia.gov/kids/energy.cfm?page=renewable_home-basics

Read reports and even write your own for the EcoReporters news section of this website at:
www.ecokids.ca/pub/eco_info/topics/renewable_energy/index.cfm

Get your eco-facts straight at:
www.eschooltoday.com/energy/renewable-energy/what-is-renewable-energy.html

Note to parents and teachers
Every effort has been made by the Publisher to ensure that these websites contain no inappropriate or offensive material. However, because of the nature of the Internet, it is impossible to guarantee that the contents of these sites will not be altered. We strongly advise that Internet access is supervised by a responsible adult.

Index

acid rain 7

biodiesel 23
biogas 24–25
biomass 22–23, 24, 28

carbon 26
carbon dioxide 7, 22, 23
chemical energy 22, 26

dams 16, 17
diesel 12, 23

electricity 4, 7, 8, 9, 10, 11,
    13, 14, 16, 17, 18, 19, 21,
    22, 25, 26, 27
electrolysis 27
emissions-neutral 7
ethanol 23

fermentation 23, 25
fossil fuels 4, 7, 22, 26, 28, 29
fuel cells 26–27

generators 14, 15, 16, 17, 18,
    19, 25
geothermal energy 20–21, 29
global warming 7, 24
greenhouse gases (GHGs) 7, 24

heat energy 4, 8, 9, 20
heat pumps 21
Helios 12
hydroelectric power (HEP) 16–17
hydrogen 26, 27

Iceland 20, 21

light energy 8, 9, 10, 11, 22

manure 6, 24, 25
methane 24, 25

NASA 12
non-renewable energy 4, 28

oilseed rape 23

passive solar design 8
petrol 23, 27
photovoltaics (PV) 10–11, 13
power stations 5, 9, 13, 17,
    21, 23

renewable energy 5, 6–7, 14,
    16, 18, 27, 28, 29
reservoirs 16, 17

Salter's Duck 19
satellites 10, 13
semi-conductors 11
silicon 11
solar-powered cars 12
solar cells 10–11, 12
solar energy 8, 9, 12
solar paint 13
solar panels 9, 11, 13
solar-powered planes 12
sulphur dioxide 7
sun 4, 6, 8–9, 10, 11, 12, 13,
    14, 22, 23, 29

Three Gorges Dam, China 17
tidal barrages 18
tides 18–19
turbines 9, 14, 15, 17, 18,
    19, 21

waste 5, 7, 24, 25, 27
water 6, 8, 9, 16–17, 18–19,
    20, 21, 23, 26, 27, 28
waves 18–19
wind power 6, 14–15, 19,
    27, 28